COLLEEN KILPATRICK

Eliminate What You Tolerate

An easy and proven way to increase your productivity, regain your focus, and liberate your energy for the more important things in life.

Copyright © 2023 by Colleen Kilpatrick

All rights reserved. No part of this publication may be reproduced, stored or transmitted in any form or by any means, electronic, mechanical, photocopying, recording, scanning, or otherwise without written permission from the publisher. It is illegal to copy this book, post it to a website, or distribute it by any other means without permission.

Colleen Kilpatrick asserts the moral right to be identified as the author of this work.

Colleen Kilpatrick has no responsibility for the persistence or accuracy of URLs for external or third-party Internet Websites referred to in this publication and does not guarantee that any content on such Websites is, or will remain, accurate or appropriate.

Designations used by companies to distinguish their products are often claimed as trademarks. All brand names and product names used in this book and on its cover are trade names, service marks, trademarks and registered trademarks of their respective owners. The publishers and the book are not associated with any product or vendor mentioned in this book. None of the companies referenced within the book have endorsed the book.

First edition

This book was professionally typeset on Reedsy.
Find out more at reedsy.com

*I dedicate this book with love and gratitude to my friend,
Katana Abbott,
and the incredible women she brought together in our Thursday
accountability group,
whose experiences and stories inspired the writing of this book:*

Gerarda

Jackie

Julie

Lynn

Marilyn

Marla

Molly

Renee

Shannon

"You get what you tolerate in yourself."

Tony Robbins

Contents

1	A Message to the Reader	1
2	Introduction	3
3	My First Experience with Tolerations	6
4	Why Do We Tolerate Stuff in Our Lives?	11
5	What Your Tolerations Are Costing You	13
6	Step 1 - Toleration Identification	16
7	Step 2 - Toleration Elimination	22
8	Benefits of Eliminating Your Tolerations	26
9	What Gives You Energy?	29
10	Success Stories	35
11	Let's Wrap it Up	39
12	Thank You and a Request	42
13	Resources	44
	About the Author	46

1

A Message to the Reader

Dear Reader,

There are thousands of books you could have purchased with your well-earned money, but you chose this one. I don't take that choice lightly. You have put your trust in me and, for this, I am grateful. Thank you.

Here's what I know for sure: the information in this book has the power to impact your life in profound ways and can do so quickly. These are some of the many benefits others have experienced from applying the technique you are about to discover:

- Personal energy increased
- Productivity improved
- Priorities clarified, goals achieved
- Anxiety diminished
- Clutter tamed or eliminated
- Organization in home and office improved
- Confidence strengthened

- Mind calmer, thinking clearer
- Feelings of accomplishment and self-mastery increased
- Focus sharpened
- Career opportunities opened
- Feelings of overwhelm reduced or eliminated
- Presence and inner peace improved
- Courage strengthened
- Relationships improved
- Joy returned

One simple technique, so many benefits. All you have to do is apply it. And when you do, I would love to hear from you. Please share your experience and successes using this technique in an Amazon review or on my Facebook page. I want to celebrate with you!

With Gratitude,
   Colleen Kilpatrick
   Milford, Michigan USA

2

Introduction

In December, 2022, my friend and colleague, Katana Abbott, a podcaster and Midlife Millionaire Coach and Founder of the Smart Women Empowerment organization, asked me to speak the following month to her online group of which I am a member. I eagerly accepted.

Since our monthly Zoom meetings are just an hour long, I wanted to share with my fellow members a topic I believed could have the greatest impact in their lives in the shortest amount of time.

I chose the topic, "Toleration Elimination", a concept created by the late Thomas Leonard, Founder of Coach University and father of the modern coaching movement. Of all the coaching techniques I had learned while studying to become a Coach at Coach U, this one was my favorite for two reasons: it brought about a quick shift in awareness in those who applied it and it provided both immediate and long-term benefits.

What exactly are tolerations? According to Leonard, tolerations are all those pesky, annoying, frustrating things we put up with - or tolerate

- in our lives. Tolerations are situations and issues that, if we had our druthers, we'd get rid of. It was Leonard's belief that tolerations hold us back in life, cause us significant grief and waste our time, attention and energy. By becoming aware of our tolerations, we could get rid of them, thus freeing up energy for bigger and better things in life.

In January 2023, I shared this information with our group on Zoom. Even before the meeting had ended, my colleagues had begun seeing their lives through a different lens where tolerations were the focus and eliminating them was the goal. Their homework was to become aware of the things they were putting up with in their lives, write them down and begin eliminating them. At the end of our 60-minutes together, I encouraged them to come to our next meeting ready to share their experience.

A month later we reconvened. Katana and I were prepared to share first in case no one else was able to do the exercise or wanted to share. You never know, right? In most groups, a portion of the people aren't able to do the work and another percentage don't care to share. But in this meeting, with this dynamic group of women, when Katana asked who had done the exercise, every hand went up. And everyone was eager to share - even our colleague, Marilyn, who was not able to join us that day. She had sent Katana an email detailing the many changes that had happened in her life in the 30-days since learning and applying this technique.

One-by-one, each woman shared a sampling of the many tolerations she had identified and eliminated in the previous month. The list of items handled by our group was long and varied and included: overdue thank you cards written; closets, drawers, cabinets and garages cleaned-out and organized; items donated; trusts drawn up; difficult conversations

INTRODUCTION

had; self-care made a priority; reunions with estranged family members enjoyed; health issues faced; medical appointments made; business forms created; business applications completed; old habits released; new, positive habits implemented; paperwork processed; employees hired; headstones for deceased loved ones completed; and the list went on.

I then asked my colleagues to share how they felt after releasing their tolerations. These are the words they used to describe their experience: "Bold", "Organized", "A sense of personal mastery", "On top of things", "My warrior emerged", "Relief", "Capable", "Confident", "A release from self-doubt", "Proud", "Liberated!". The best part was that each woman shared her personal successes with elevated energy, immense enthusiasm and a big smile on her face.

Their experiences and stories touched and inspired me deeply. It had been years since I led a workshop on this topic or hosted a Toleration Elimination Virtual Party, but seeing the changes in my colleagues that day, reminded me of the transformative power of this simple process. At the end of our virtual gathering, I made a decision. The book you hold in your hands is a result of that decision. It is an expanded version of the information I shared with my colleagues that day. May it bless your life.

> "When you change the way you look at things,
> the thinks you look at change."
> Max Planck, 1858-1947, Quantum physicist

3

My First Experience with Tolerations

It was on a road trip through southern Utah twenty-five years ago that I first learned of the budding personal coaching industry. My sweetheart, Ben, and I had stopped at a little grocery store in St. George, Utah to pick-up a few supplies for our camping adventure in nearby Zion National Park. Standing in the checkout line, I spotted a magazine headline that piqued my interest and, ultimately, changed the direction of my life. I don't remember the headline, but I clearly recall the contents of the article. It was about personal coaching, a profession that is extremely common today, but unheard of outside of the sports arena back then. In reading the article, I became very intrigued with the idea of becoming a personal coach. Soon after I returned from that vacation, I enrolled in Coach University and began taking classes after work in the event photography studio I operated with Ben.

As part of my training to become a coach, I hired my first coach. Following our introductory call, my new coach sent me a welcome packet which included a variety of worksheets she asked me to complete and return to her before our next session. I eagerly filled out every one of them - except one. It was titled, "What Are You Tolerating?".

MY FIRST EXPERIENCE WITH TOLERATIONS

Under the headline, at the top of the worksheet, was a short explanation:

"We humans have learned to tolerate so many things. We put-up with, accept, and are dragged down by people's behavior, situations, broken or missing belongings, unmet needs, unfinished business, crossed boundaries, annoyances, problems and even our own behavior. You are tolerating more than you think. Take a couple of minutes to write down everything you sense you are tolerating."

When I read that description and saw 80 empty spaces on the worksheet, I naively and rather arrogantly thought, "No way! Who tolerates 80 different things at one time? Not me. I don't put up with stuff that bugs me. I deal with it. I can't think of three things to add to that list."

I was in for a rude awakening.

That night, back in the log cabin I shared with Ben, I set the coaching packet on the kitchen island and began to prepare dinner. I hoped that I would be able to think of a few tolerations I could put on the list and call it "done".

As I was chopping vegetables, I noticed, once again, that I was straining to read the recipe I was following. At that time, the only light in the kitchen was from a pendant light that hung from the cathedral ceiling above and behind me. The problem was that no matter where I was working in our little L-shaped kitchen, that light cast a shadow of my torso onto my workspace. I always felt like I was working in the dark, because I was. The lack of light and the inability to see in a space I spent a lot of time, was a big and daily frustration for me. I looked behind me and up at that light and thought to myself, "Ah-hah! I have my first toleration!"

As I was writing "poor lighting in kitchen" down in slot #1 on the worksheet, my eyes fell on my favorite black, double-breasted blazer hanging near the front door. Because black clothing is the uniform of choice for event photographers, that blazer was the hardest-working piece of clothing I owned. It was beautifully made and perfectly tailored, but it had issues. It was missing the inside button and on a double-breasted blazer, that's a problem. In order to ensure that the blazer hung properly on me, I had to somehow secure the inner panel. In the absence of a button, I did that with a large safety pin. And every time I wore it, I'd have to futz with that darn pin. It was annoying and time-consuming, but I tolerated it. For months! So, #2 on the list, "Missing button on black blazer".

In discovering those first two tolerations, my awareness shifted. I suddenly understood what tolerations were and, soon after, exactly what they were costing me.

Later that evening, I walked around our home looking at our living environment with new eyes. We had so much to be grateful for about that first home of ours: the remote, off-the-grid location, the charm of a log cabin and the unobstructed views from the spacious deck. But the list of things we were tolerating in our new home was very, very long.

For starters, in the winter months, the inside temperatures rarely got above 42 degrees Fahrenheit which meant we lived in that house for several months each winter with coats, hats and gloves on most of the time. (The irony is that as I type this manuscript, I am sitting in my Michigan home with coat, hat, and fingerless gloves on. A February ice storm came through the area and knocked out the power grid, and with it, heat. Turns out, life off-the-grid back then was good preparation for power outages now!)

MY FIRST EXPERIENCE WITH TOLERATIONS

When we bought our Nevada home in the mountains above Las Vegas a year prior, we had no clue what we were in for or how cold and windy it could get at 6500 feet elevation. We also had no idea that the house was intended to be a summer home to escape the heat of the valley below. Consequently, it had no central heating. The two tiny pellet stoves that were meant to take the chill off a spring evening, just couldn't keep up with the volume of air, the height of the ceilings, the large windows, and the freezing overnight temperatures of winter in the mountains. To make matters worse, the gaps in the chinking between the logs allowed every icy breeze to blow in and through the house. Some mornings, there was ice in the dogs' water dishes - inside the house! Being cold all the time was a huge toleration.

As if that weren't bad enough, our two cars, although perfect for our long highway commute, were not equipped for the snowy, icy roads in and around our mountain village. Here's what that meant: After working until the wee hours taking photos at swanky Las Vegas events, we'd go back to the studio, unload our photography equipment, feed our dogs, change from work attire into mountain attire, load up the car with groceries and supplies, drive 45 freeway miles toward our home, then an additional 14 miles on an unlined and unlit road until we arrived at the entrance of the village. But, because our cars couldn't handle the steep, icy roads within the village, we had to park our car next to the paved road and hike the last 1.5 miles to our home - often at 1:00 or 2:00 in the morning. Some nights we pulled a sled filled with groceries and supplies up and down those hilly roads through biting wind, ice and snow only to arrive, dead-tired, at our freezing cold, unheated home. And when the day had been cloudy with no sun to charge the solar panels, there was no electricity and no lights.

Crazy, right?

Crazier still, was the fact that I didn't see all those things as the tolerations they clearly were - at first. Needless to say, as I became aware of all that I was tolerating in the house and beyond, that first worksheet with space for 80 entries filled up real fast.

> **"Small ills are the fountains of most of our groans.**
> **Men trip not on mountains, they stumble on stones."**
> Chinese Proverb

4

Why Do We Tolerate Stuff in Our Lives?

At a recent dinner party, a friend of mine mentioned to a few guests that I had lived off-the-grid in the mountains of Nevada. Hearing that, one of the men asked to know more. I told him a little bit of what I just shared with you. He looked at me with the most quizzical expression on his face and said, "Why the heck would you put up with that?" I laughed! "Good question!" And, for sure, I had heard it before.

As I mentioned earlier, Ben and I loved our mountain lifestyle, but there were trade-offs, just as there are in all of life. The fact is, there are a number of reasons we humans put up with stuff that go far beyond mere trade-offs. Here are some of the most common:

1. We've become numb to the issue, so much so, that it doesn't even occur to us to deal with it. In our mind, it's just the way it is. (This was definitely me back then.)

2. We are in a state of overwhelm. Just getting through the day takes everything we've got. We have no extra energy or attention to focus on anything beyond the absolute necessities of life.

3. We believe it is easier to ignore the problem than do something about it.

4. We assume the solution is going to require way too much time, money or effort to resolve, so we don't look into it or make it a priority. (This was me, too!)

5. We're scared. Some of the big tolerations in life require a lot of courage to handle and we just don't feel up to the task.

The truth is, I've ignored tolerations for every one of the reasons listed above. No doubt, we all have. But when you really understand what your tolerations are costing you, you become braver and bolder and more eager to deal with them head-on.

"Action precedes motivation."
Robert McKain

5

What Your Tolerations Are Costing You

Little or large, the things that bother you day-in and day-out have a huge cost. For starters, they clutter your mind and slow your thinking. That's because they're always running in the background whether or not you're consciously aware of them. Imagine your tolerations as open programs on your computer. The more programs you have open, the slower the processing.

Tolerations also keep you from being fully engaged in the present moment. It's difficult to pay attention to what's going on right in front of you or engage fully in conversations with loved ones, clients or colleagues when you're distracted by thoughts about things that are annoying or troubling you.

And the bottom line is, tolerations deplete your life force energy and consume the very energy you need to bring your finest dreams and goals to life.

To really understand the toll tolerations take on you, consider this short, but impactful expression Tony Robbins often shares in his seminars:

"Where attention goes, energy flows."

When we stop to ponder it, we realize that we truly do give away a little - or a lot - of our energy to everything that vies for our attention. At the end of the day, that adds up to a lot of lost energy. It's no wonder we feel "spent".

In his book, "Why Your Life Sucks and What You Can Do About It", self-help guru and best-selling author Alan Cohen writes:

> **"Energy is like currency. While you may be very careful about what you pay for with your cash, you are probably far less careful about what you pay for with your attention. In the long run, how you spend your attention affects your life far more profoundly than how you spend your money."**

Everything in your life, every single thing you do and every action you take, requires a little bit of your attention and, thus, costs a little bit of your energy. But, what you may not realize at first, is that the actions you *don't* take and the tasks you *don't* do, consume your attention and energy, as well. Every time you contemplate what you're going to say in that conversation you've been putting-off or every time you think about the doctor's appointment you haven't made for the health issue that isn't going away, you spend your energy.

Over time, that adds up to a big loss of life force. And as we all know, when our personal energy is low, everything in life seems more challenging. Just getting through the day is a chore. Worse yet, our most creative ideas and our most inspired dreams appear unattainable, unable to come to life without our special spark.

WHAT YOUR TOLERATIONS ARE COSTING YOU

Often when we're in a low-energy state, the first thing we consider is what we should add to our life or do more of to increase our energy such as, get more sleep, drink more water, exercise more, eat more healthy food, spend more time with uplifting, energizing people, etc. No doubt, each of these things can help and all are important. But, often, a more effective approach is to first take a look at all the things in your life that drain your energy and, then, eliminate them.

Coach and Speaker, Cheryl Richardson, puts it this way in her book, "Take Time for Your Life":

> "A high quality life has more to do with what you remove from your life, than what you add."

Such was the case with my client, Bev, a successful businesswoman and mother of two. Bev came to me for assistance and support in creating a plan of action to achieve several personal and professional goals. Confident, feisty and intelligent, Bev was blessed with many qualities that contributed to her success except one...energy.

Feeling frustrated, unfocused and overwhelmed much of the time, Bev was finding it nearly impossible to be and do all that she desired. Before developing a plan of action that would have required even more of her energy to implement, we decided to first concentrate our coaching on increasing her personal energy.

This is how we set-out to improve Bev's life force energy...

6

Step 1 - Toleration Identification

"Respect yourself enough to walk away from anything that no longer serves you, grows you or makes you happy."
Unknown

The process I shared with my coaching client, Bev, that I now share with you, requires awareness, action and persistence but can be reduced to this simple formula:

Subtract from your life the things that drain your energy.
Add to your life the things that give you energy.

The first half of the formula - subtracting the things that drain you - can be mastered in two steps. Identification and Elimination.

Step 1 - Toleration Identification

In this first step, simply become aware of the things you are tolerating. Pay attention to what frustrates, agitates or annoys you in your daily life. Where are you procrastinating? What are you putting up with that you

STEP 1 - TOLERATION IDENTIFICATION

would change if you could?

As Bev discovered in her first experience with this exercise, tolerations can be ordinary, seemingly insignificant things such as a missing drawer handle, or a thank-card that needs to be written, or an oil-change that is long overdue.

Bev also discovered that tolerations can involve significant, weightier issues such as a relationship that is no longer working, a crazy, relentless schedule, and a job that no longer provides any challenge.

The easiest way to discover your tolerations is to look for them in these 6 key areas of life:

<u>Environment</u> - Each time I create a new Tolerations List, I start with my living space and I encourage you to do the same. Looking for tolerations in your environment makes your first foray into toleration discovery much easier because you'll have visual clues and tangible reminders of things that annoy you. Here are some common tolerations that can be found in and around our homes:

- Clutter
- Disorganized closets, drawers, rooms, garage
- The lack of something: privacy, reading lights, storage, the right furniture
- A space that longer fits your lifestyle
- Unfinished projects
- Lack of private outdoor space

<u>Possessions</u> - Our belongings are next up in our toleration search. As with our environments, tolerations having to do with our possessions

are easy to identify.

- Outdated or missing clothing/jewelry/shoes/accessories
- Clothes that need mending
- Broken belongings
- Supplies and equipment for hobbies, sports and activities you no longer do
- A vehicle that needs repairing, cleaning or replacing
- Gifts, purchases, inherited items you keep out of guilt
- Items that have a negative charge or memory attached to them

Body, Mind and Spirit - While pondering tolerations in this category, many people soon become aware of health issues and concerns that have been running just under the surface of their conscious awareness. This is a great opportunity to bring those concerns to light and make self-care a bigger priority in your life.

- Personal habits - rushing, smoking, drinking, eating fast, sleeping in, going to bed late, spending inordinate amounts of time looking at a screen
- An unhealthy diet
- Low water intake
- Lack of exercise
- Lack of self-care
- No time for hobbies or joyful pursuits

Career / Business - Consider your feelings toward your work and career. Do you wish you had more responsibility? Less? Has the idea of starting your own business or working from home been on your mind for years? Remember, what we dream of doing, starting and creating, if not acted upon, becomes a toleration, too.

STEP 1 - TOLERATION IDENTIFICATION

- A stressful or unfulfilling job
- Being overworked/underpaid
- A long commute
- Ineffective filing system - physical and/or electronic
- Not enough business/too much business
- Outdated skills
- Outdated professional headshot

Finances - No matter your financial situation, this is an area of tolerations for most. Identifying and eliminating financial frustrations in your life can bring about significant peace of mind as well as ever-increasing abundance.

- Lack of awareness of your current financial situation
- Debt
- No savings plan
- Dependency on one source of income
- Disorganized financial documents
- No trust or will

Relationships - Acknowledging tolerations in the way we relate to others or others relate to us, can be extremely difficult, but ruminating about unresolved relationship issues can be far worse. Consider if you are tolerating any of the following:

- Other people's behavior/comments/habits
- Your behavior within a relationship
- Weak personal boundaries
- Unfinished business
- Lack of desired relationships or community

As you become aware of your tolerations in the 6 key areas of life, be sure to write them down. Start a dedicated list or write them in a journal where you can add and subtract tolerations and track your progress over the long-haul. Keeping track of tolerations in writing is an essential step. By capturing them on paper, you take the things that have been nagging or annoying you and move them from the back of your mind to the front. Once you become fully aware of all that you've been putting-up with, you'll be eager to take action and start crossing them off your list one-by-one.

Don't fret if your first pass at identifying your tolerations produces meager results. That's normal. Most of us have become numb to the things in our life that bother us. Trust that a seed of awareness has been planted in your mind and will soon take hold. When it does, you will look at all aspects of your life through a new lens.

Keep your Tolerations List handy and your awareness engaged as you train your mind to become aware of all that you're putting up with in life. Maintaining a paper list is great, but some, like me, prefer to keep their toleration list as a pinned note on their phone so it's always available. Whichever way works best for you, continue adding to your list. Chances are good you'll get hooked on this simple technique for upgrading your life.

As you move through the identification step, you may become aware of a toleration that seems too huge or too costly to handle. If that happens, first, give yourself credit for recognizing it for what it is. It takes courage to admit that an important aspect of your life is not working for you. When you're ready, add it to your list and trust that a solution will come to you in perfect time. Awareness and receptivity will make it far more likely that you notice possible solutions as they present themselves.

STEP 1 - TOLERATION IDENTIFICATION

Once your awareness of your tolerations is established and growing, you'll be eager to begin the next step to this powerful technique: Toleration Elimination.

"Don't waste a single second on anything that doesn't nourish your soul."

Zianna's Mom

7

Step 2 - Toleration Elimination

"You don't have to see the whole staircase, just take the first step."
Martin Luther King Jr.

With your Toleration List in hand, it's time to launch into resolving and eliminating the things you've been putting up with one-by-one. Here are some pointers that will make the process easier.

Start Small. For me and many others, starting small is the ticket. When you make that phone call you've been putting-off or write the email you've been resisting, you'll immediately feel a sense of relief and a surge of energy. Although seemingly inconsequential, the little tasks we don't do consume our energy every time we think about them, dread them or chastise ourselves for not doing them. Once the task is completed, all that misdirected energy is freed up for bigger and better things. Not only will your energy increase when you deal with the little issues head-on, so will your confidence and feelings of self-mastery all of which will inspire you to eliminate more and bigger tolerations on your list.

STEP 2 - TOLERATION ELIMINATION

Start Big. Some people are of the mindset, "Go big or go home!". They want to handle their biggest tolerations right out of the gate. Sometimes those biggies are what are called "Pivotal Tolerations" and getting rid of them immediately resolves several other things you've been putting up with. For example: getting a higher-paying job you can do from home that is more in line with your strengths could resolve the tolerations of a long commute to a job you don't enjoy, for pay that is less than what you're worth - all in one fell swoop.

Continue Adding and Deleting from Your List. In the weeks, months and years ahead, stay vigilant to new and recurring tolerations in your life. The faster you deal with them, the less energy you'll give them and the more energy you'll have for creating the life you truly desire. Consider updating your tolerations list at the start of every month, quarter or year, then continue adding and subtracting from your list regularly as you strive for a toleration-free life.

As you begin eliminating your tolerations, you may come up against a little or a lot of internal resistance that keeps you from taking action. For me, sometimes that's fear, other times it's feelings of overwhelm. Either way, as soon as I feel resistance and identify my reason for inaction on any given issue, I strive to shift my thinking by using the following expression I learned from a very wise mentor and colleague, Jordan Adler of SendOutCards.

Here's the expression:

"_____ takes me out of action; action takes me out of _____."

Into those two blanks go the reason for my inaction, for example:

"**Fear** takes me out of action; action takes me out of **fear**."

Then, I say the whole thing to myself or right out loud. It's a powerful reminder that all I need to do is take one step in the direction of my desire and trust that my fear will dissipate, my courage will grow and my path will be made clear. I have learned that, more often than not, my anticipation of a task is far worse than the actual task. So, by taking the first step and getting into action, any anticipatory anxiety I may have felt just thinking about the task, often just goes away.

I've modified the saying above to include other common reasons we humans have for avoiding or ignoring undesirable tasks.

"**Doubt** takes me out of action; action takes me out of **doubt**."

"**Anxiety** takes me out of action; action takes me out of **anxiety**."

"**Overwhelm** takes me out of action; action takes me out of **overwhelm**."

"**Procrastination** takes me out of action; action takes me out of **procrastination**."

The key to remember is this: our reason for **inaction**, can often be overcome with **action**.

Now it's your turn. What is your go-to reason for avoiding uncomfortable tasks? Write it down in the two blanks below.

"_____ takes me out of action; action takes me out of

STEP 2 - TOLERATION ELIMINATION

_____."

I encourage you to commit your personalized mantra to memory and say it to yourself, or right out loud, whenever resistance shows up in the Toleration Elimination phase. It will swiftly guide you back into action.

8

Benefits of Eliminating Your Tolerations

> "When we conquer fear, we conquer many.
> Conquering becomes our habit.
> When we avoid fear, we avoid many.
> Avoiding becomes our habit."
>
> Unknown

We all know how good we feel after we make an appointment we've been putting off or how relieved we feel when we finally get our taxes filed. Not only do we feel more energetic, we feel calmer and less burdened. Eliminating the things you've been tolerating will give you a noticeable boost in energy as well as a feeling of personal mastery, both of which will enable you to take on bigger, more important goals and dreams.

Suggestions for Multiplying the Benefits of Toleration Elimination

Set a Goal to Eliminate 3 or More Tolerations Each Week. If you want to upgrade your life, energy and thinking quickly, consider making the elimination of tolerations part of your weekly game plan. Note them on your "To-Do" list and schedule them into your calendar. Keep in mind that an uptick in energy, confidence and self-mastery will be your reward. For extra incentive, promise yourself a reward of the tangible or experiential kind after handling a difficult toleration. For me, that looks like a new quart of paint for my next furniture restoration project after cleaning out my filing cabinet or lunch with a friend after getting my taxes done.

Get an Accountability Partner. Find a friend or colleague also on a personal development path who wants to fast-track their transformation. Share this book with them. Teach them this process. Then, agree to meet weekly to discuss the tolerations you've each identified and the successes you've both experienced. Having an Accountability Partner is one of the best ways to stay committed on your path to a toleration-free Life.

Make it a Group Project. When the elimination of tolerations becomes a company or family project, the results can be exponential. Consider asking your co-workers / employees / family members / friends / accountability group / Book Club to join you in a Toleration Elimination Project. Have them all list what they're tolerating and set a time frame of a week or a month for handling them. Then, agree to check back with one another for sharing and support. Not only will you get to know and be able to support your fellow members in new ways, you'll experience a significant increase in your personal and collective energy. In the process, you'll surely discover new ideas and inspiration for upgrading your own life.

As an example, when one of the partners from our Thursday accountability group mentioned that she was tolerating not having a trust and the uneasiness she felt whenever she imagined the chaos it would cause her family in the event of her passing, I realized I was tolerating the very same thing – both the lack of a trust and the uneasiness it caused me. So, onto my Toleration List went, "Lack of a personal trust".

In the next moment, my accountability partner was inspired by the "before" and "after" photos I shared of my newly transformed spice cabinet after I had identified it as a daily – albeit, less significant – toleration. So, onto her list went, "Disorganized and outdated Spice Cabinet".

Being accountable to others on the Toleration Elimination journey will help you stay the course and make the journey more interesting and inspiring. Celebrate each other's victories and enjoy the collective rise in energy and enthusiasm you all will experience!

9

What Gives You Energy?

When I think back to the Toleration Elimination worksheet I was asked to complete by my first coach, I now understand why I hesitated to fill it out. In my limited thinking, the exercise seemed to be asking me to focus on everything that was wrong in my life. That did not feel comfortable. In fact, the whole toleration exercise seemed to run counter to everything my loving, optimistic, "be thankful for your blessings" Mother had taught and demonstrated for me. On the other hand, writing in my Gratitude Journal every night...now that felt comfortable.

And what about the expression, "What you think about, you bring about"? I wondered, "Wouldn't I just get more of the same if I spent time focusing on everything that annoyed and frustrated me instead of what I was grateful for?"

I stayed in that quandary of inaction until the moment I realized, once again, that I was straining my eyes to read a recipe due to the poor lighting in my kitchen. That's when the light bulb went on (pun intended). I got it! As much as I believe in having a daily gratitude practice, no amount of entries in my Gratitude Journal would have allowed me recognize the many frustrating and annoying things I was tolerating in my life. Without awareness, I would not have taken action. Without action, nothing would have changed. Over time, the pages of my Gratitude Journal would have become full of all the blessings in my life, while my personal energy would have been squandered on the many things I was putting-up with.

In the beginning of this book, I shared a list of the benefits I and others have experienced from eliminating tolerations. In position number one on that list is an increase in personal energy. It is the greatest of benefits from doing this work because energy is everything. It is essential for life. With it, we can do so much. Without energy, we lack the get-up-and-go to bring our best self or our best ideas to the world.

The idea of having more energy to do the things you really enjoy and be the best you can be, is a powerful motivator on the path to a toleration-free life. As you let go of activities, jobs, commitments, tasks, habits and things that no longer serve you, you'll experience not only more energy but more spaciousness - both in your environment and your calendar. When that happens, I encourage to keep this bit of wisdom in mind:

"Nature abhors a vacuum."
Aristotle

No doubt, when the ancient Greek Philosopher, Aristotle, made this observation back in the 4th Century B.C., he wasn't thinking about tolerations, but he certainly could have been. It definitely applies.

The website www.freedictionary.com provides a modern spin on that ancient axiom which goes like this:

"Any absence of a regular or expected person or thing will soon be filled by someone or something similar."

No doubt, you and I have experienced this phenomenon in a variety of ways such as...

- you clear the clutter from your drawer/garage/car/refrigerator/shelf/purse/wallet and in no time, it fills back in.
- you resign from serving on a board and soon after you receive an invitation to serve on another board.
- you clear Friday afternoon on your schedule for self-care, and it becomes the go-to time slot for anything that didn't make it on your schedule between Monday and Friday.

The good thing is that when we eliminate even the smallest of frustrations from our lives, we create space for other things. Ideally, better things, but that's not always the case. Sometimes what comes back into our lives is more of the same.

There is solution. It requires you to become very selective about what you allow back into the empty spaces you've just created. Like a museum curator who decides which treasures to keep, which treasures to pass on and which new treasures to allow in, you become the curator of your own life. You get to decide what stays, what goes, and what you allow in.

The job of curating your own life promises to be much easier if you get crystal clear about what lights you up. This is essential, for in the absence of clarity, you may be inclined to fill the gaps with things, relationships, opportunities and commitments that aren't right for you and the new life you're creating.

Here's a simple way to gain the awareness and clarity you need to curate the next, best chapter of your life.

Years ago, I attended a series of workshops led by my friend, Suzanne Young, a Law of Attraction Coach. In one of the sessions she asked each of us to simply make a list of the things we love to do including the activities and events that energize us. At the time, I was mourning the loss of both my parents after having partnered with my sister in their care over an extended period. Thinking about activities and events that energize me was about the furthest thing from my mind. As it turned out, every other woman in that workshop was in a similar situation. In the process of becoming dependable, responsible, hard-working female adults, we had each marginalized our our own self-care and joy to one degree or another.

The exercise Suzanne gave us, although straightforward, was not so easy to do at first, but, with a bit of coaxing and some good emotive music, we remembered the activities that lit us up. Here are some them:

- spending time in nature
- hiking in the woods
- enjoying time with grandchildren
- attending a sporting or theatrical event with friends
- canoeing and kayaking
- taking photographs
- creating art
- riding a bike
- going on a road trip
- morning walks
- dancing
- gathering around a fire with friends

- meeting friends and family for a meal and conversation
- gardening
- making music
- making bouquets of flowers for neighbors and friends
- re-purposing old furniture
- hosting a game night
- enjoying a scented bath by candlelight
- water color painting

To every women in attendance, that exercise was an eye-opener. The simple act of focusing on and writing down our favorite things, brought long-forgotten interests to our minds and smiles to our faces. But, more importantly, the exercise helped us realize how little time and attention we had been giving to those special things in life that brought joy to our hearts and nourished our souls. With our new awareness, we were encouraged to prioritize our lives differently making room for all that we love.

Maybe, you too, have been adulting for so long that you've forgotten what it is you really love to do. I trust this exercise will give you the same degree of awareness and clarity it gave us. Give it a try. Think about what brings you joy? What do you love to do? What activities put a smile on your face and a bounce in your step? If you're stumped, think back to what you loved to do as a child. Notice what comes up for you. Make a list so you never again forget what brings you joy.

Now, the essential step: select something you've identified that energizes you and invite it into your life. Bring it into your environment or add it to your calendar. Make it a priority. When you know with certainty what you love, you'll be more inclined to fill in the gaps created by resolved tolerations with only those things that give you energy. As your energy expands, not only does your life improve, but so does every life you touch.

**"Passion is energy.
Feel the power that comes from focusing on what excites you."**

Oprah Winfrey

10

Success Stories

Fresh Fuel for the Pursuit of Bev's Dreams

After our initial meeting, my client Bev, the creative thinker with big dreams and a lot of confidence mentioned earlier, made a list of everything that was annoying or frustrating her. She was surprised to discover that her list was long and varied and touched on every area of her life.

Next, I asked her to begin eliminating these energy drains one-by-one. Each week at the beginning of our call, we reviewed her progress. The result for Bev was profound. She immediately felt an increase in personal power, vital energy and joy. Once she discovered how energizing it was to eliminate her most obvious tolerations, she felt motivated to look for and eliminate even more. As her energy increased, her confidence grew as did her desire to take bolder action in the pursuit of her dreams and ideas.

By example and results, Bev inspired her family, friends and colleagues to live by this formula:

> **Subtract from your life the things that drain your energy.**
> **Add to your life the things that give you energy.**

My Garage Gets a Makeover

Last spring, I updated my list of tolerations and identified my garage as a big source of ongoing frustration for me. A single-car garage built in 1950, it had become cluttered and disorganized. Worse was the fact that it was very dark inside from the brown, aged, unfinished wood that formed its structure. I so disliked pulling into it - especially at night. In doing this exercise, I realized something that surprised me. While my husband was alive, that dark garage didn't bother me because, I suppose, I knew that his warm welcome awaited me. But after he died, having that dreary garage as the first thing I saw every time I returned home, triggered sadness and grief. That was a revelation to me and I wanted to do something about it. As soon as I added "Dark, disorganized garage" to my toleration list, I began planning its makeover.

By the end of the summer, my garage had undergone a total transformation including a clearing of clutter, the addition of bright, white paint to all the walls, a new, organized space for recycling and trash, white peg board on the side walls with a hook for every tool and garden implement, framed art on the back wall and new lighting which included a string of black party lights around the upper perimeter. Now when I pull into the garage, especially at night, the space feels festive and welcoming and I feel joyful and peaceful inside. I still miss my husband's warm welcome, but pulling into my garage no longer triggers grief.

Zach's Business Tolerations

My client, Zach, runs a design and branding studio. He and his team are very good at what they do, but like many business owners he often felt overwhelmed, overworked and underpaid. The energy and enthusiasm he once had for his business had diminished, and because of that, he was having a difficult time keeping up with his work and attracting high-caliber clients.

One of the first things I asked Zach to do was to make a list of the things that were bothering or frustrating him at work.

What Were Some of Zack's Business Tolerations?

- Informational clutter
- An overflowing in-basket and stacks of paper on the floor
- A backlog of emails
- An inadequate system for handling inquiries from new clients
- A receptionist who was unfriendly and lacked a can-do attitude
- Rushed breakfasts and no time for lunch
- Haphazard marketing that cost him a lot and wasn't getting him the results he wanted

How Zach's Tolerations Affected Him

Reviewing Zach's List with him, I asked how his tolerations made him feel. This is what he shared with me:

- "From the minute I arrive at the office, I feel like I'm behind the eight ball."
- "I always have this nagging feeling that things are out of control and I'll never be able to catch-up."
- "I worry that something is going to fall through the cracks any

- minute – or it already has."
- "I feel overwhelmed and distracted much of the time."
- "I find myself cringing when a new client calls because I can hardly handle the amount of work I have now."

Zach had so many significant, energy-sucking tolerations, it was no wonder his enthusiasm for his work had vanished. But once Zach was crystal clear about his work tolerations and the toll they were taking on him, he needed no encouragement to start eliminating them.

A month later, I stopped by his office to check-in. Not only was Zack's energy more effervescent, the energy in the entire office was elevated. The space felt lighter, more orderly; calmer, yet electric. Best of all, Zack reported that by eliminating some of the significant things he had been tolerating in his business, he was feeling more confident in his and his colleagues' abilities to deliver fabulous service to his clients. Best of all, his enthusiasm for his business and his creativity had returned. He was very excited to fill me in on all the new opportunities coming his way.

> **"Give power to the solution, not the problem."**
> Unknown

11

Let's Wrap it Up

Back to the Cabin

For most, creating their first Toleration List can be quite revealing. As I mentioned earlier, the majority of people discover they've been tolerating 80 to 100 things when they create their first Toleration List.

Keeping a current Toleration List can ensure greater clarity, focus and results over the long term - especially important for any multifaceted undertakings like running a business or maintaining a home.

Looking back, as Ben and I became aware of the things we were tolerating in our log home, we realized that most would require significant time, effort and resources to overcome. There were no quick fixes. So, as we could, each thing we tolerated in those early days was resolved and eliminated from our list. Ben still lives in that house we once shared, but his Toleration List is much shorter. Today the home has central heating, abundant lighting, thicker chinking between the logs and a 4-wheel drive vehicle in the driveway.

The elimination of tolerations is not a static process. As you eliminate some tolerations, new ones appear. But, with your new awareness of tolerations and the cost they carry, you will recognize them earlier, before they become a serious drain on your energy and your happiness.

You now have a simple formula for transformation that is straightforward, fast-acting and effective.

Subtract from your life the things that drain your energy.
Add to your life the things that give you energy.

As we know, this information will benefit you only if you use it constructively. If you close this book and think to yourself, "Sounds like a great idea!" or "I don't put up with things that bother me!" (as I did) and do nothing more, you will not experience the life transforming benefits this formula has been proven to deliver. Knowledge must be applied effectively and efficiently to be useful in creating change.

My Challenge for You

So, here's my challenge for you. Before you do anything else, while you're pondering what you've just learned, take a few minutes to identify 10 or more things you've been reluctantly putting-up with in your life. Consider what you're tolerating in the 6 key areas of life mentioned in Chapter 6 and make a quick list of them. Next, choose three or more tolerations you will eliminate this week - or even today. Schedule them right into your calendar. Do the things you need to do to take care of them. Then, pay close attention to how you feel once those tolerations have been resolved. If you're like most, you'll feel more energized and confident with a greater sense of well-being, all essential for achieving loftier goals and dreams. Imagine what it would be like to experience those positive feelings every day. You can, by making the elimination of tolerations a priority in your life.

"**You are what you repeatedly do. Excellence is not an event, it's a habit.**"

Aristotle

12

Thank You and a Request

Dear Reader,

Thank you for choosing to read my book, "Eliminate What You Tolerate". I sincerely hope you found it helpful. If you enjoyed the book, I would be grateful if you could take a moment to leave a positive review on Amazon. Your honest feedback will not only help others decide if this book is right for them, but it will also help me write future books. I look forward to hearing your thoughts on this book as well as the successes you experience as you eliminate your tolerations.

Thank you so much for your support!
   Colleen Kilpatrick

THANK YOU AND A REQUEST

"No one else can speak the words on your lips
Drench yourself in words unspoken
Live your life with arms wide open
Today is where your book begins
The rest is still unwritten"

From the song, "Unwritten" by Natasha Bedingfield

13

Resources

CoachVille. (2023, January 18). *ICF Certified Coaching Program – Life Coaching Program and Community.* https://coachville.com/

Cohen, A. (2005). *Why Your Life Sucks: And What You Can Do About It* (Reprint). Bantam.

Idioms and phrases. (n.d.). TheFreeDictionary.com. https://idioms.thefreedictionary.com/

Jordan Adler. (2017, August 27). Jordan Adler. https://www.jordanadler.com/about

Katana Abbott Midlife Millionaire® Coach and Financial Planner. (2022, June 13). Katana Abbott Midlife Millionaire® Coach. https://katanaabbott.com/

Natasha Bedingfield. (n.d.). Natasha Bedingfield. https://www.natashabedingfield.com/

Richardson, C. (2023). *Take Time for Your Life: A Seven-Step Programme for Creating the Life You Want* (First Edition). Bantam Books.

Smart Women's Financial Empowerment | Find Your Financial Freedom. (2020, December 22). Smart Women's Financial Empowerment. https://smartwomensempowerment.org/

Suzanne Young | Personal Success Programs. (n.d.). https://psprograms.com/suzanne/

Tony Robbins - The Official Website of Tony Robbins. (2019, March 21). tonyrobbins.com. https://www.tonyrobbins.com/

About the Author

Colleen Kilpatrick is a speaker, author and creative collaborator. In her work with other entrepreneurs, Colleen draws upon her unique and varied background in marketing, business innovation, personal development and spiritual teachings to inspire people to bring their best gifts to the world. The creator of Business Brainstorming Sessions, Toleration Elimination Virtual Parties and numerous business and personal development programs, Colleen is known for her ability to turn complex concepts into simple, step-by-step solutions that can be understood and implemented with ease.

You can connect with me on:
 https://www.facebook.com/colleen.t.kilpatrick

Made in the USA
Columbia, SC
23 April 2023